Personal Finance

By

KARL BIEDENWEG, Ph.D.

COPYRIGHT © 1999 Mark Twain Media, Inc.

ISBN 1–58037–091–8

Printing No. CD–1326

Mark Twain Media, Inc., Publishers
Distributed by Carson-Dellosa Publishing Company, Inc.

Table of Contents

Introduction

This book was designed to introduce the student to the many areas of personal finance. Most of the topics covered are not new concepts for the students, but the majority of students have never applied these concepts to their personal lives. After a brief overview of each topic area, the student is asked to complete hands-on assignments. Further, there are suggestions for guest speakers at the end of most chapters. Guest speakers can give extra insight into the topic area along with exposing the student to different career opportunities.

The beginning chapters address career choices and income. This is followed by basic banking issues, such as checking and savings accounts. Next, protecting what you have is examined. The importance and types of insurance are discussed. Investment options are explored in the following chapter. The different types of stocks, bonds, and related issues are examined. The next chapters deal with planning, budgeting, and borrowing money to finance major purchases, such as automobiles and houses. The final chapter covers various types of taxes and their impact on U.S. taxpayers.

After reading the book and completing the assignments, students should have a good personal finance foundation to build on. Furthermore, students should realize that financial security does not happen by itself; everyone needs to set financial goals and have a plan to accomplish those goals.

I finally know what distinguishes me from the other beasts: financial worries. —Renard

Chapter 1: Career and Income Goals

This book deals with personal finance, that is managing one's own or one's family money. Unless we inherit our fortune or win the lottery, most of us need to work in order to have an income large enough to satisfy at least our basic needs and wants. In this chapter, we will discuss career choices and income goals.

Do you know what you want to do after finishing your education? It is very important that you have some idea of what you would like to do as a **career**. If you know what you want to do, then you can make sure to take the right courses in school. You can also expose yourself to situations and experiences that will benefit your career choice.

Probably the most important thing in determining **career satisfaction** is enjoying what you do. If you dread going to work on Mondays and only look forward to the weekends, you will be unhappy five-sevenths of your working life. By evaluating your personal experiences and taking advantage of the various career-oriented preference tests, you can better understand what career is likely to be satisfactory for you.

If you enjoy what you are doing, you will probably succeed at it. Handsome **financial rewards** usually come with success. If you look at the people you know who are financially well off, you will see that they have a passion for their given career.

It is almost impossible to satisfy every career objective you have set. If a job is easy and fun, it may not challenge you to grow. If a job does not require personal mobility (moving around the country), you will lack the diversity that geographic experiences can bring. If a career is exceedingly popular, there will probably be more qualified applicants than jobs available, thereby keeping a lid on salaries.

Even though it is sometimes very difficult to choose among different careers, putting time and effort into the process usually pays off in the long run. Most people give little thought to career choice—they just drift along the path of least resistance until they find themselves trapped in an unsatisfying career. Those who give careful, long-range thought to career choice are likely to be much more satisfied than those who do not.

Have you ever given any thought to the "meaning of life" and what you need to do in order to achieve it? Everyone seeks different things from life. There was a popular bumper sticker a few years ago that stated, "He Who Collects the Most Toys Before He Dies WINS." Although this bumper sticker was humorous, the vast majority of people seek other rewards from life. Unfortunately, many people do not give this subject much thought until they are close to dying, and then it is usually too late to make adjustments in their lives. Just like making career plans so you can expose yourself to situations that will benefit you, you also need to give some overall thought to **what you want to achieve in life outside of your career**, so you can get into positive situations, find mentors, and reach the financial level needed to achieve your goals.

Name_____ Date _____

Chapter 1: Student Activities

GUEST SPEAKER IDEA

Invite the placement/career center director from a local college to speak to the class. This individual's job is to help college graduates get jobs in their career areas. Many college students are unsure about what they want to do for a living, and the director has a series of exercises and tests that can indicate the students' interests.

STUDENT ACTIVITIES

1. What are at least two reasons why people should think about what they want to do upon graduation from high school or college?

   a. _____

   _____

   b. _____

   _____

2. What are some situations or experiences that students can expose themselves to that will benefit them in their career choices?

   a. _____

   b. _____

   c. _____

   d. _____

3. Write a short paper on what you think the "meaning of life" is all about. What type of career and income level will afford you the opportunity to accomplish your stated "meaning of life"?

Name_____ Date _____

CLASS ACTIVITY

Have the students write down several career objectives, either that they have or that they know others have. In a round-robin fashion, have each student express a career objective. The teacher or another student should list the objectives on the board as they are given. From this expanded list, have each student choose the ones that are the most important to him or her. Have each student write a short paper explaining why these chosen objectives are important to him or her and then have him or her find or choose a career(s) that will achieve those objectives.

1. Write your career objectives below.

    a._____

    _____

    b._____

    _____

    c. _____

    _____

    d._____

    _____

2. After reviewing the list of objectives on the board, select the ones that are most important to you.

    a._____

    _____

    b._____

    _____

    c. _____

    _____

    d._____

    _____

Name_____ Date _____

Chapter 1: Crossword Puzzle

Use the clues on page 6 to complete the crossword puzzle about careers and income goals.

Name_____ Date _____

Chapter 1: Crossword Puzzle Clues

Use the clues below to complete the crossword puzzle on page 5. Answers may be found in the chapter on career and income goals.

ACROSS

1. Since all career objectives are difficult to achieve, most people need to make _____ .

3. Many people follow the career that offers the path of least _____.

5. If you enjoy what you are doing, you will probably _____ at it.

10. If you are unsure about a suitable career, _____ tests are available.

11. Most people give little thought to their career _____.

13. This book deals with personal _____.

14. You know that you are in the perfect career if you _____your work.

DOWN

2. The more one plans for a career, the more likely one will be _____.

4. A career should be _____.

6. One variable in choosing a career path is favorable past _____.

7. Success usually brings handsome financial _____ .

8. An experienced person who acts like a role-model and gives you guidance is a _____ .

9. Personal finance is the management of one's own _____.

10. Most people who are financially successful have a _____ for their work.

12. What we desire to do for a living is our _____.

Chapter 2: Checking Accounts

What Is a Check?

A **check** is a written order to your bank. It tells the bank to take a stated amount of money from your account and pay it to another individual or business.

Reasons for Opening a Checking Account

- Checks are safer to carry around than cash. If your checks are stolen, you can put a "stop payment" on them, keeping them from being charged to your account.

- Checks serve as proof of payment if the payee has endorsed (signed the back of) the check.

- If you pay your bills by mail, you have no proof of payment if you send cash. A check provides proof of payment.

- You can establish good credit by properly maintaining your checking account. A good credit reference will come in handy when applying for a credit card or loan.

- By using a checking account, you can keep track of your income and expenses, which will help you budget your money.

Checking Accounts

One of the safest and easiest ways to manage your money is through a checking account. Soon you will begin working and earning an income, and as you begin to accumulate material goods, such as computers and automobiles, you will have bills to pay. The easiest way of paying and keeping track of what you have paid is by using your checking account. By paying with a check, you have a permanent record of the payment if it ever comes into question. You also have a record of payment for tax purposes, and checks eliminate the need to carry large amounts of cash when paying bills or shopping. Further, by reviewing your check register, you can tell exactly how much you spend on certain items each month, which is very helpful in developing a budget that will help you reach your financial goals.

Signature Card

When you open a checking account, you will be asked for personal identification and also to fill out a signature card. The purpose of the signature card is to protect you and your money in case of forgery or robbery. If the bank teller is unfamiliar with the person cashing the check, he or she might compare your signature (hopefully) on the check to your signature on your signature card, or the teller might ask the person trying to cash the check some personal questions asked on your signature card (such as your date of birth) to verify the person trying to cash the check has the right to do so.

Ownership of Account

☐ Individual   ☐ Partnership   ☐ Checking   ☐ Savings
☐ Joint*   ☐ Corporation (For Profit) ☐ Certificate of Deposit ☐ Money Market
☐ Proprietorship   ☐ Corporation (Not for Profit) ☐ NOW Account   ☐ IRA
☐ Other _____
☐ Trust - If in Trust: ☐ New   ☐ Existing
                                                ☐ Other _____
Beneficiary _____
Address _____   Business Employer _____
                                                        Business Address _____
☐ Payable on Death – If payable on death:
Beneficiary _____
Address _____   Business Phone _____

* Joint Accounts WROS Agreement - The Joint Account Customers that have signed this Agreement below acknowledge that they are the owners of this account as joint tenants with the right of survivorship and not as tenants in common, and upon the death of any one Customer, the balance shall become property of the survivor(s). If two or more Customers shall be the survivors, their interests shall continue to be as joint tenants with the right of survivorship. All sums presently or hereafter deposited in this account shall be the property of the customers jointly, and upon receipt of proper order, payable to any one of the customers. Each Customer agrees to be jointly and severally liable for any deficits in the account, regardless of which Customer created such deficit.

Initial Deposit _____
Name _____
Address _____
_____ Date Opened _____
Phone _____ Number of Signatures Required _____
applies for an account with   ACCOUNT NO.

YOUR HOMETOWN BANK
HEREIN REFERRED TO AS "BANK"

1. _____
   Authorized Customer Signature   S.S. or I.D. No.
2. _____
   Authorized Customer Signature   S.S. or I.D. No.
3. _____
   Authorized Customer Signature   S.S. or I.D. No.
The above Customers, whether one or more, are herein referred to as "Customer."

By signing below, Customer 1) agrees to the conditions on both sides of this card; 2) authorizes Bank to recognize the above signature(s) for transaction of business in this account; 3) acknowledges that they have received a copy of Bank's current Funds Availability Policy; and 4) certifies under penalties of perjury, (a) that the number shown on this form is their correct taxpayer identification number and (b) that they are not subject to backup withholding either because they have not been notified that they are subject to backup withholding as a result of a failure to report all interest or dividends, or the Internal Revenue Service has notified them that they are no longer subject to backup withholding. The Internal Revenue Service does not require your consent to any provisions of this document other than the certifications required to avoid backup withholding.

A. _____   B. _____   C. _____

Checking Account Deposits

Before you write a check, you must deposit money into your account. When you deposit money into your account, you first fill out a deposit slip. On the deposit slip you indicate how much in cash and how much in checks you are depositing. Also, on the deposit slip there is a space labeled "Less Cash Received." This is the money you would like back before the deposit.

DEPOSITED WITH

YOUR HOMETOWN BANK

DATE _____ 19 ____

Account No. [ ][ ] ⦙⦙⦙ [ ][ ][ ][ ]

Checks and other items are received for deposit subject to the terms and conditions of this bank's collection agreement. Deposits may not be available for immediate withdrawal.

NAME _____

ADDRESS _____

CITY _____

	DOLLARS	CENTS
CURRENCY		
COIN		
CHECKS (List Separately)		
TOTAL OF CHECKS LISTED ON BACK		
LESS CASH RECEIVED		
TOTAL DEPOSIT		

Writing Checks

Now that you have money in your checking account, you can write checks. There are some basic rules you should use when doing so.

1. Always use ink so that no one can change your numbers.

2. Print and write your numbers clearly so there are no misunderstandings.

3. Do not change the way you sign your name.

4. If you make a mistake, write "VOID" on the check and use the next check.

```
┌──────────────────────────────────────────────────────────────────┐
│  Jane Smith                                    No. 1234            │
│  111 River Road                                                    │
│  Hometown, USA                                      80-817/815     │
│                                          Date _____    │
│                                                                    │
│  Pay to the order of _____ $[          ]     │
│                                                                    │
│  _____ DOLLARS               │
│                                                                    │
│  YOUR HOMETOWN BANK                                                │
│                                                                    │
│  MEMO _____   _____                │
│  |: 0815081781 :    "·012 345"·    1234                            │
└──────────────────────────────────────────────────────────────────┘
```

It's called "cold cash" because it's never in your pockets long enough to get warm.
—Unknown

Name_____ Date _____

REVIEW QUESTIONS

1. What are some good reasons why we should use checks instead of cash?

_____

_____

2. Why do banks require you to fill out a signature card before opening your account?

_____

_____

LET'S PRACTICE WHAT WE HAVE LEARNED

1. Fill out the following "Signature Card."

Ownership of Account

☐ Individual	☐ Partnership	☐ Checking	☐ Savings
☐ Joint*	☐ Corporation (For Profit)	☐ Certificate of Deposit	☐ Money Market
☐ Proprietorship	☐ Corporation (Not for Profit)	☐ NOW Account	☐ IRA

☐ Other _____

☐ Trust - If in Trust: _____   ☐ New   ☐ Existing

Beneficiary _____   ☐ Other _____

Address _____

_____   Business Employer

☐ Payable on Death – If payable on death: Business Address

Beneficiary _____   _____

Address _____   Business Phone

*Joint Accounts WROS Agreement - The Joint Account Customers that have signed this Agreement below acknowledge that they are the owners of this account as joint tenants with the right of survivorship and not as tenants in common, and upon the death of any one Customer, the balance shall become property of the survivor(s). If two or more Customers shall be the survivors, their interests shall continue to be as joint tenants with the right of survivorship. All sums presently or hereafter deposited in this account shall be the property of the customers jointly, and upon receipt of proper order, payable to any one of the customers. Each Customer agrees to be jointly and severally liable for any deficits in the account, regardless of which Customer created such deficit.

Initial Deposit _____

Name _____

Address _____

_____ Date Opened _____

Phone _____ Number of Signatures Required _____

applies for an account with   ACCOUNT NO.

YOUR HOMETOWN BANK
HEREIN REFERRED TO AS "BANK"

1. _____   _____
   Authorized Customer Signature   S.S. or I.D. No.

2. _____   _____
   Authorized Customer Signature   S.S. or I.D. No.

3. _____   _____
   Authorized Customer Signature   S.S. or I.D. No.

The above Customers, whether one or more, are herein referred to as "Customer."

By signing below, Customer 1) agrees to the conditions on both sides of this card; 2) authorizes Bank to recognize the above signature(s) for transaction of business in this account; 3) acknowledges that they have received a copy of Bank's current Funds Availability Policy; and 4) certifies under penalties of perjury, (a) that the number shown on this form is their correct taxpayer identification number and (b) that they are not subject to backup withholding either because they have not been notified that they are subject to backup withholding as a result of a failure to report all interest or dividends, or the Internal Revenue Service has notified them that they are no longer subject to backup withholding. The Internal Revenue Service does not require your consent to any provisions of this document other than the certifications required to avoid backup withholding.

A. _____ B. _____ C. _____

Name_____ Date _____

2. Suppose you wanted to deposit some birthday money. If your brother gave you $0.50, your uncle gave you $5.00, your aunt gave you a check for $10.00, your grandparents gave you a check for $25.00, and you wanted $8.00 back to go to the movies, fill out the following deposit slip to show the correct information.

DEPOSITED WITH		DOLLARS	CENTS
YOUR HOMETOWN BANK	CURRENCY		
	COIN		
DATE_____19___	CHECKS (List Separately)		
Account No. [ ][ ] ▥ [ ][ ][ ][ ]			
Checks and other items are received for deposit subject to the terms and conditions of this bank's collection agreement. Deposits may not be available for immediate withdrawal.			
NAME_____			
ADDRESS_____	TOTAL OF CHECKS LISTED ON BACK		
	LESS CASH RECEIVED		
CITY_____	**TOTAL DEPOSIT**		

3. Many people cause confusion because they misspell the numbers on their checks. Correctly spell the following numbers. If you are unsure, use a dictionary.

a. 4 _____   b. 8 _____

c. 10 _____   d. 11 _____

e. 12 _____   f. 13 _____

g. 14 _____   h. 15 _____

i. 18 _____   j. 19 _____

k. 20 _____   l. 23 _____

m. 30 _____   n. 34 _____

o. 40 _____   p. 45 _____

q. 50 _____   r. 56 _____

s. 60 _____   t. 67 _____

u. 70 _____   v. 78 _____

w. 80 _____   x. 89 _____

y. 90 _____   z. 100 _____

Name_____ Date _____

    aa. 113   _____

    bb. 748   _____

    cc. 1000   _____

    dd. 1009   _____

    ee. 1783   _____

    ff. 2000   _____

    gg. 2313   _____

    hh. 2999   _____

4. Let's say you went to Barney's Music Shop and bought some used CDs. Fill out the following check for $13.48.

Name: _____   No. **1234**

Address: _____   80-817/815

_____

_____   Date _____

Pay to the order of _____ $ [   ]

_____ **DOLLARS**

    YOUR HOMETOWN BANK

MEMO _____   _____

| : 0815081781 :   ".012 345".   1234

---

5. You would like to order a poster from a mail order company called Wall-To-Wall Poster Company. Fill out the following check for $8.95.

Name: _____   No. **1235**

Address: _____   80-817/815

_____

_____   Date _____

Pay to the order of _____ $ [   ]

_____ **DOLLARS**

    YOUR HOMETOWN BANK

MEMO _____   _____

| : 0815081781 :   ".012 345".   1235

Keeping Your Check Register

The check register is where you record the checkbook transactions. There is a place for the check number, date, transaction description, and the amount, along with a column for a running total. There are several types of checkbook transactions that can be recorded besides the writing of a check. Other types of transactions might include a charge for new checks, a bank service charge, an automated teller machine (ATM) transaction (explained in more detail later), or a routine deposit.

Reconciling Your Checking Account

Your financial institution will typically send you a statement every month. On this statement they will list all your checks the bank has received for payment, all the deposits they have received on your account, ATM withdrawals, interest earned, and any other transactions made in your checking account during the month.

There are many reasons why what you think you have in your checking account may be different than what the bank says you have in your account. The individual or business that you wrote a check to may not have cashed or deposited your check yet, the bank may have assessed a service charge to your account, or you may have earned interest that you have not added to your account. Whatever the reason for the difference, it is important you **reconcile** or agree with the difference. If the difference cannot be reconciled, then that means that either you or the bank has made a mistake. Typically on the back of the bank statement there is a Reconciliation Form, or you can use the simple eight-step method listed below.

Eight-Step Method to Reconcile Your Checking Account

1. Put a check mark beside every transaction in the check register that matches to the entries on the statement.

2. List in the check register and subtract all fees charged to your account.

3. List and total all checks that you have written but that have not cleared your account.

4. List and total all deposits that you have made but that are not shown on the statement.

5. List the balance shown on the statement.

6. Add deposits (Step 4) to the balance.

7. Subtract outstanding checks (Step 3) from the balance (Step 6).

8. The check register total should now match the reconciled amount (Step 7).

ATMs or Automated Teller Machines

ATMs are computerized banking machines. ATMs are located at convenient locations to make your banking activities easier. Most routine banking can be done at an ATM. You can deposit, withdraw, and transfer money from one account to another. The major advantage of ATMs is that they are available 24 hours a day, 365 days a year.

In order to access your banking account via an ATM, you need an ATM card. You usually apply for this card the same time you open your checking and savings accounts. Although the plastic card looks like a credit card, in most cases it can only be used for ATM transactions. When you receive your ATM card, you will also receive a secret Personal Identification Number, better known as a PIN. With your card and PIN, you can use most ATMs, although certain banks' ATMs have a fee you must pay if you are not a member of the bank. (By law, the machine must notify you of any additional fee.) When you use an ATM, it is your responsibility to record the transaction in your check register or in your savings passbook.

A typical ATM transaction would go something like this. (Note: Although similar, most ATMs differ in steps and language.)

Step 1	Insert your card into the ATM.
Step 2	The machine will ask for your PIN. Using the keyboard, enter your secret PIN.
Step 3	The ATM will ask you to select a transaction from a list of possibilities. Using the up and down keys, select one and push enter.
Step 4	The ATM will ask you for the amount of your transaction. Using the keyboard, enter the dollar amount.
Step 5	The ATM will acknowledge that this transaction has been completed and ask if you would like to perform another transaction.
Step 6	If you do not wish to perform another transaction, hit the NO prompt.
Step 7	The ATM will give you the money requested and/or a receipt of your transaction and your card will be returned.

Name_____ Date _____

Chapter 2: Student Activities

Two months of checking transactions are listed in the following activity. Correctly enter the transactions into the check register and reconcile your bank statement for each month.

Transactions for the Month of May

May 2	Opened your checking account with a deposit of $50.00
May 3	Wrote check 101 to Bill's Shoe Store for $16.15
May 5	Wrote check 102 to General Telephone for $32.45
May 7	Deposited paycheck for $245.32
May 7	Wrote check 103 to Dr. Jones for $28.00
May 9	Wrote check 104 to Bargain-Mart for $64.81
May 11	Wrote check 105 to Adams Electric for $84.63
May 12	Wrote check 106 to Sally's Beauty Salon for $28.00
May 14	Deposited paycheck for $245.32
May 15	Wrote check 107 to First Mortgage for $200.00
May 18	Wrote check 108 to Style's Dept. Store for $19.56
May 21	Deposited paycheck for $245.32
May 24	Wrote check 109 to The Gas Company for $72.84
May 25	VOIDED check 110 (made a mistake in writing check)
May 25	Wrote check 111 to Ace Telemarketing (Elvis CDs) for $24.67
May 28	Deposited paycheck for $245.32
May 31	Received bank statement.
	Reconcile your statement using the following information.

Name_____ Date _____

CHECK REGISTER			DEBITS (-)		✓	CREDITS (+)		BALANCE	
NUMBER	DATE	DESCRIPTION OF TRANSACTION	CHECKS FEES			DEPOSITS		$	

Name_____ Date _____

May 1 Through May 31

Checking Account Bank Statement

Beginning Balance 00.00		Ending Balance 237.52	
Deposits/Credits 785.96		Checks/Debits 548.44	

	CHECKS/DEBITS	DEPOSITS/CREDITS	BALANCE
5-2		50.00	50.00
5-3	16.15		33.85
5-5	32.45		1.40
5-7		245.32	246.72
5-7	28.00		218.72
5-9	64.81		153.91
5-11	84.63		69.28
5-14		245.32	314.60
5-15	200.00		114.60
5-18	19.56		95.04
5-18	28.00		67.04
5-21		245.32	312.36
5-24	72.84		239.52
5-31	2.00 service charge		237.52

Name_____ Date _____

Bank Statement Reconciliation

Follow the eight-step method presented earlier.

Step 1   Put a check mark beside every transaction in the check register that matches to the entries on the statement.

Step 2   List in the check register and subtract all fees charged to your account.

Step 3   List and total all checks written that have not cleared your account.

Step 4   List and total all deposits not shown on the statement.

Step 5   List the ending balance shown on the statement.

Step 6   Add deposits (Step 4) to the ending balance.

Step 7   Subtract outstanding checks (Step 3) from the balance (Step 6).

Step 8   Check register total should match the reconciled amount (Step 7).

If the check register and reconciled amount do not match, go through the eight-step process again (be very careful that the numbers are correct).

Check List If Your Account Does Not Balance

• Have you correctly entered the amount of each check in your register?

• Have you correctly entered the amount of each deposit in your register?

• Have you correctly entered the amount of other transactions in your register?

• Have you recorded all service charges and deducted them in your register?

• Have you carried the correct balance forward when beginning a new page in your register?

• Have you checked all addition and subtraction in your checkbook register and on the statement reconciliation?

• Have you accounted for all of your outstanding checks in your reconciliation?

Name_____ Date _____

Transactions for the Month of June

June 1   Wrote check 112 to Miller's Grocery for $87.23

June 2   Wrote check 113 to Ted's Video Store for $7.87

June 3   Deposited paycheck for $245.32 less $50.00 cash

June 5   Wrote check 114 to General Telephone for $37.41

June 6   Wrote check 115 to Office Supply Co. for $7.37

June 9   Wrote check 116 to Adams Electric for $78.87

June 10   Deposited paycheck for $245.32

June 12   Withdrew $30.00 from ATM

June 14   Wrote check 117 to First Mortgage for $200.00

June 15   Wrote check 118 to Fashion Plate Boutique for $132.23

June 17   Deposited paycheck for $245.32

June 17   Wrote check 119 to Miller's Grocery for $35.56

June 18   Wrote check 120 to Ray's Hardware for $8.55

June 23   Wrote check 121 to The Gas Company for $69.65

June 25   Wrote check 122 to Sally's Beauty Salon for $38.00

June 26   Wrote check 123 to the *Daily Times* for $13.87

June 28   Wrote check 124 to Style's Dept. Store for $144.34

June 30   Received bank statement.

                Reconcile your statement using the following information.

Name_____ Date _____

June 1 Through June 30

Checking Account Bank Statement

Beginning Balance	237.52	Ending Balance	289.18
Deposits/Credits	931.28	Checks/Debits	879.62

	CHECKS/DEBITS	DEPOSITS/CREDITS	BALANCE
6-1		245.32	482.84
6-1	87.23		395.61
6-2	7.87		387.74
6-2	24.67		363.07
6-3		195.32	558.39
6-5	37.41		520.98
6-6	7.37		513.61
6-9	78.87		434.74
6-10		245.32	680.06
6-12	30.00 ATM withdrawal		650.06
6-14	200.00		450.06
6-15	132.23		317.83
6-17		245.32	563.15
6-17	35.56		527.59
6-18	8.55		519.04
6-23	69.65		449.39
6-26	13.87		435.52
6-28	144.34		291.18
6-30	2.00 service charge		289.18

Name_____ Date _____

Bank Statement Reconciliation

Follow the eight-step method presented earlier.

Step 1   Put a check mark beside every transaction in the check register that matches to the entries on the statement.

Step 2   List in the check register and subtract all fees charged to your account.

Step 3   List and total all checks written that have not cleared your account.

Step 4   List and total all deposits not shown on the statement.

Step 5   List the ending balance shown on the statement.

Step 6   Add deposits (Step 4) to the ending balance.

Step 7   Subtract outstanding checks (Step 3) from the balance (Step 6).

Step 8   Check register total should match the reconciled amount (Step 7).

If the check register and reconciled amount do not match, go through the eight-step process again (be very careful that the numbers are correct).

Chapter 2: Crossword Puzzle

Name_____ Date _____

Use the clues on page 23 to complete the crossword puzzle below about checking accounts.

Name_____ Date _____

Chapter 2: Crossword Puzzle Clues

Use the clues below to complete the crossword puzzle on page 22. Answers may be found in the chapter about checking accounts.

ACROSS

2. If you make a mistake on a check, you should write the word _____ on it.
4. Good credit is important when you want to apply for a _____.
6. A written order to your bank is called a _____.
8. Banks use the signature card to verify your _____.
10. Checks serve as proof of payment if the check has been_____.
11. By paying with a check, you have a permanent _____ of your payment.
12. Some banks may charge a _____ to use their ATM.
13. By properly maintaining your bank account, you can establish good _____ .
16. Checks are a safe and easy way to pay your _____ .
17. Checks eliminate the need to carry large amounts of cash when_____ .
18. ATM stands for automated teller _____.
19. PIN stands for personal identification _____.

DOWN

1. If your checks are stolen, you can put a "stop _____" on them.
3. Always fill your checks out using _____ so the numbers cannot be changed.
5. When you open a checking account, you will be required to fill out a _____ card.
7. Checks are safer to carry around than _____.
9. By using your checking account, you can track your income and_____.
11. You record checks written and deposits made in your check_____.
14. After receiving a statement from the bank, you should _____ your checking account.
15. When you deposit money into your checking account, you need to fill out a deposit _____.

Chapter 3: Savings Accounts

What Is a Savings Account?

A **savings account** is an account at a bank in which you deposit money and earn a certain amount of interest on that money. A savings account at a bank is a very safe place to keep money that you may need in the short term or money you want to keep available for emergency situations. The main reason why savings accounts are used for short-term investments is because they pay a minimal interest rate compared to other types of investments. Bonds, for example, will typically pay a much higher rate for a longer time period. However, bonds take longer to mature and there are sometimes penalties for early withdrawal.

Opening a Savings Account

To open a savings account, you first choose a bank you want to do business with. You may take into consideration the location of the bank and the interest rate offered by the bank. Then you need to visit the bank and speak with the person in charge of setting up new accounts. He or she will have you fill out a personal information sheet listing some information about you and anyone you wish to have access to your account. You will also have to fill out a signature card similar to the one discussed in the chapter on checking accounts. To open your account, the bank will require you to make a minimum deposit, usually $10 or $20. Then you will be issued a **passbook**. The passbook is typically a small, firm paper booklet in which the bank will record all your deposits and withdrawals. You will need to bring the passbook with you every time you want to make a deposit or withdrawal.

Interest earned on the money in your account will also be recorded in the passbook. The next time you make a transaction after the interest period has ended, the interest will be posted to your account. For example, if interest is paid to savings account holders on March 31, it will not be posted to your passbook until you make your next deposit or withdrawal.

Specialized Savings Accounts

There are many specialized savings accounts that have been established by banks to compete against other higher-interest investments. These specialized accounts typically pay higher interest rates, but there are restrictions attached to them. Some restrictions may include having to maintain a high minimum balance or restrictions on when you can make withdrawals. Some common examples of these specialized accounts include Now Accounts, Super Now Accounts, Christmas Club Accounts, and Cash Management Accounts.

Name_____ Date _____

Chapter 3: Student Activities

In the following exercises, assume that you have deposited the specified amounts in your savings account. Calculate the interest you would earn for the specified time periods and interest rates.

Calculating Simple Interest:

Principal x Interest Rate x Time = Interest

Note: Time is measured in years or fractions of years.

1. You deposit $250 in your savings account. How much would be in your account in three years if you earned three percent interest and the interest was added to your account once a year? (Hint: Add in the interest for each year prior to calculating the interest for the following year.)

   _____ the first year

   _____ the second year

   _____ the third year

2. You deposit $250 in your savings account. How much would be in your account in three years if you earned six percent interest and the interest was added to your account once a year?

   _____ the first year

   _____ the second year

   _____ the third year

3. You deposit $600 in your savings account. How much would be in your account in four years if you earned five percent interest and the interest was added to your account once a year?

   _____ the first year

   _____ the second year

   _____ the third year

   _____ the fourth year

Name_____ Date _____

4. You deposit $75 in your savings account. How much would be in your account in 10 years if you earned four percent interest and the interest was added to your account once a year?

_____ the first year

_____ the second year

_____ the third year

_____ the fourth year

_____ the fifth year

_____ the sixth year

_____ the seventh year

_____ the eighth year

_____ the ninth year

_____ the tenth year

5. You deposit $100 dollars in your account at five percent yearly interest. At the end of every year, you post the interest to your account, and then you deposit another $100. How much money will be in your account at the end of five years?

_____ the first year

_____ the second year

_____ the third year

_____ the fourth year

_____ the fifth year

Name_____ Date _____

Chapter 3: Crossword Puzzle

Use the clues on page 28 to complete the crossword puzzle below about savings accounts.

Name_____ Date _____

Chapter 3: Crossword Puzzle Clues

Use the clues below to complete the crossword puzzle on page 27. Answers may be found in the chapter about savings accounts.

ACROSS

2. To open a savings account, you will be required to fill out a_____ card.

5. In a_____Club Account, you make regular deposits all year to save money for the holidays.

6. When you make a _____ or withdrawal, it is recorded in your passbook.

8. Savings accounts are used for short-term investments because they pay _____ interest rates compared to other types of investments.

9. The _____ is a small, firm paper booklet in which the bank will record all your deposits and withdrawals.

13. A savings account is a safe place to keep money for _____ situations.

15. A _____ account is an account at a bank in which you deposit money and earn interest on that money.

DOWN

1. While bonds pay a higher rate of interest than savings accounts, there are sometimes_____ for early withdrawals.

3. There are many _____ savings accounts established by banks to compete against other higher-interest bearing investments.

4. There may be restrictions on specialized accounts about when you can make _____.

7. Specialized savings accounts may pay higher interest rates, but they may have _____ attached to them.

10. Some specialized savings accounts may require a high minimum_____.

11. The money the bank pays you for keeping your money in a savings account is called _____ .

12. Interest will not be _____to your account until you make your next transaction.

14. An example of a specialized savings account is a Super_____Account.

Chapter 4: Insurance

Insurance is an important part of your personal finances. **Property insurance** is used to keep one from experiencing major losses of the material things that one has been able to accumulate, such as automobiles, furnishings, and houses. **Life insurance** is designed to help cover lost wages and to pay important expenses in case an unexpected death occurs.

Let's take a closer look at the basic types of insurance and the variety of coverages from which one can choose.

Auto Insurance

Roads and highways are getting more crowded than ever these days. The more people drive, the greater their chances are of being involved in an accident. Many states require that all drivers carry auto insurance (usually some type of liability coverage). There are six basic types of auto coverage.

1. **Bodily Injury Liability:** provides money to pay claims against you and the cost of your legal defense if your car injures or kills someone.

2. **Property Damage Liability:** provides money to pay claims and defense costs if your car damages the property of others.

3. **Medical Payments Insurance:** pays medical expenses resulting from accidental injuries. Covers you and your family as well as other passengers in your car.

4. **Uninsured Motorist Protection:** pays for injuries caused by an uninsured or a hit-and-run driver.

5. **Collision Insurance:** pays for damage to your car resulting from a collision or overturning.

6. **Comprehensive Physical Damage Insurance:** pays for damages when your car is stolen or damaged by fire, flood, hail, or other perils.

Deciding Which Coverages You Need

Here are three points to consider before buying automobile insurance.

1. YOUR FINANCIAL RESPONSIBILITY. Every driver has a responsibility not only for driving in a safe manner, but also for injuries or damages he or she might cause. Most states have laws that make it mandatory that you have some level of coverage. The amount of the claim may well exceed the amount of coverage you have, which means that the claimant has the right to seek payment from your personal assets. This is truly something to consider in determining the type and amount of coverage you need.

2. YOUR AUTOMOBILE. If you drive an older model, its value might seem low compared to the cost of collision coverage. In this case, you may decide not to buy collision insurance.

3. YOUR PERSONAL FINANCES. Collision and comprehensive coverages are available with a **deductible**. This means that the car owner agrees to pay a specified amount ($100, $200, or $500) for the damage to his or her car in each loss and the insurance company agrees to pay the remainder. By eliminating the cost of processing small claims, the company can provide coverage at a lower price. Consequently, the higher your deductible, the lower the cost of the insurance.

Life Insurance

There are two basic types of life insurance: term insurance and universal insurance.

TERM INSURANCE. People generally choose to buy term insurance when they have something in particular that needs to be financially protected for a specific period of time. For example, if you have a $100,000 home mortgage for 20 years, you could buy decreasing term insurance, which would pay off the mortgage in case of your death.

Term policies are usually much less expensive than universal life policies. If you are of limited means, term insurance is a good option. Furthermore, universal insurance accumulates value over the years, but if you have other financial means of saving for retirement, term insurance might better suit your needs.

The one major drawback of a term life insurance policy is that it only provides coverage for a specified period of time. When the policy term ends, the insured person does not receive any benefits from the policy. This is similar to renting an apartment versus buying a house. When you leave your apartment, you have no equity value.

UNIVERSAL LIFE INSURANCE. Most people prefer to buy universal life insurance because of the long-term advantages. Some universal life policies accumulate funds that can be used to cover expenses during retirement, pay off a mortgage early, pay for children's college education, or save for an emergency fund.

One of the major advantages of a universal life policy is you get lifetime coverage, and you also accumulate cash value over the years. Usually, the cash value begins to grow after the first few years of the policy, allowing you to use the cash value for other things. This is what makes universal life an attractive policy for savings purposes.

A universal life insurance policy is generally more expensive during the early policy years than a term policy because of the long-term advantages and the accumulation of cash value.

Sample Life Insurance Application:

LIFE INSURANCE APPLICATION

1. Insured (Print)_____ ☐M ☐F

2. Address_____

   City_____ State_____ Zip_____

3. Social Security Number_____

4. Telephone Number (   ) _____

5. Date of Birth _____ Age Last Birthday _____

6. Height _____ ft._____ in. Weight _____ lbs.

7. ☐ Basic Plan _____ Amt. $ _____
   ☐ Flex. Prem. Annuity Rider - Prem. $_____ Ann.

8. Premium _____
   Premium Payable: ☐ Ann. ☐ S.A. ☐ Quar. ☐ PAC
   Is Automatic Premium Loan Option to Apply? ☐ Yes ☐ No

9. Primary Beneficiary   Relationship

   Contingent Beneficiary   Relationship

10. Owner, if other than the Proposed Insured
    Name_____ Age _____
    Relationship_____
    No. & Street_____
    City_____ State_____ Zip_____
    Soc. Sec. or Tax ID No. of Owner _____

11. Has the Proposed Insured, during the past 10 years, been treated for or been diagnosed as having Acquired Immune Deficiency Syndrome (AIDS)?   Yes ☐   No☐

12. Has the Proposed Insured received treatment at a hospital or been disabled in the past 18 months, or received treatment or been advised to receive treatment for cancer in the past 18 months, or had a heart attack in the past 18 months? (If yes, give details.)   ☐ Yes ☐No

13. Has the Proposed Insured had an application for life or health insurance rejected, postponed or cancelled within the past 6 months?   ☐ Yes ☐No

14. Please give details to questions 11 through 13 (if answered yes). Include doctors' names, addresses, dates and other details.

15. Will proposed insurance replace any existing policy or annuity? If yes, which?   ☐Yes ☐No

16. Special Requests

For Home Office Endorsement

The statements and answers on the front of this Application Part One are true and complete to the best of my knowledge and belief. It is agreed that (a) this application and any amendments hereto, with the answers made to the medical examiner and recorded on Part Two, if a medical examination is required by the Company, shall be the basis of any insurance granted; (b) no agent or medical examiner has authority to waive the answer to any question in the application, to pass on insurability, to waive any of the Company's rights or requirements or to make or alter any contract; (c) acceptance of any policy issued shall constitute ratification of any endorsements in the space entitled "For Home Office Endorsement," except that no change in the amount, classification, plan of insurance or annuity, or benefits shall be effective unless agreed to in writing by the Applicant, and (d) except as may be provided in the conditional receipt bearing the same number as this application, no insurance or annuity shall be considered in force unless and until a policy shall have been issued by the Company and said policy manually received and accepted by the Applicant and the full first premium paid thereon, all during the lifetime and before any change in the insurability of any person proposed for insurance from that stated herein.

The Company shall have sixty days from the date hereof within which to consider and act on this application and if within such period a policy has not been received by the Applicant or if notice of approval or rejection has not been given, then this application shall be deemed to have been declined by the Company.

AUTHORIZATION: I authorize any licensed physician, medical practitioner, hospital, clinic, medical or medically related facility, insurance company, medical information bureau, or other organization, institution or person that has records or knowledge of the health of me, to give to _____ Insurance Company or its Reinsurers such information. A photocopy of this Authorization shall be considered as valid as the original.

I have paid the sum of $ _____ with this Application. Dated at _____ this _____ day of_____ 19 ___

_____
Signature of Applicant (in full)
Proposed Insured (if under 15, parent or guardian signature)

_____
Signature of Proposed Insured

AGENT'S STATEMENT: Is insurance being applied for intended to replace any insurance now in force? ☐ YES ☐ NO
I have truly and accurately recorded in this Application, the information supplied by applicant.

Form 10948   _____   _____
                                          Licensed Agent   Agent #

Name_____ Date _____

Chapter 4: Student Activities

GUEST SPEAKER IDEAS

1. Invite an independent insurance appraiser to discuss the various ways he or she goes about trying to value personal property existing in a home prior to a loss.

2. Invite a spokesperson from the local police department to talk to your class about how they might prevent a loss from burglars.

3. Invite an insurance agent to discuss the types of homeowners and life policies available and under what circumstances they should be obtained.

STUDENT ACTIVITIES

1. A personal property inventory is noting your personal property along with original costs and age of each item or group of items. There are several reasons why everyone should complete a personal property inventory.

   a. It records how much personal property was purchased for (important whether or not property is insured for replacement cost or market value).

   b. The record will reinforce claims to the insurance company because it will document the existence and value of any item that might be lost or damaged.

   c. The personal property inventory is typically done for each room, thus, identifying where items of value are located in the home (this enables one to know exactly what has been lost or destroyed in any given area of the house).

   d. Using the information from the inventory, valuables can be distributed evenly throughout the house, thereby reducing the possibility of an unduly large loss in any one area of the house.

   Using the form on page 33, each student should complete a personal property inventory of one room in his or her home. Students are usually surprised by the volume and cost of goods located in the room.

Name_____ Date _____

Personal Property Inventory

Room in House: _____

Item Description	Purchase Date	Original Cost

Name_____ Date _____

Chapter 4: Crossword Puzzle

Use the clues on page 35 to complete the crossword puzzle below about insurance.

Name_____ Date _____

Chapter 4: Crossword Puzzle Clues

Use the clues below to complete the crossword puzzle on page 34. Answers may be found in the chapter about insurance.

ACROSS

2. The type of coverage that pays the claim against you if your car damages the property of another is property damage _____.

6. The type of coverage that pays for injuries caused by an uninsured driver is _____ motorist protection.

8. The type of coverage that pays the claim against you if your car injures or kills someone is_____ injury liability.

11. The type of coverage that pays medical expenses resulting from an auto accident is _____ payments insurance.

13. A claimant has the right to seek additional money from your personal _____.

14. To protect our material things, we purchase this type of insurance.

_____

15. The type of life insurance that is purchased for a specific period of time is referred to as _____.

DOWN

1. You may decide not to buy collision insurance if you drive an _____ model automobile.

3. Since highways are getting busier, we are at a greater risk of becoming involved in an auto _____.

4. To help compensate for lost wages and to cover important expenses in case unexpected death occurs, we purchase _____ insurance.

5. The type of coverage that pays for damage to your car resulting from a collision is _____ insurance.

6. The type of life insurance that is purchased as an investment is referred to as _____.

7. An important part of your personal finances is _____.

9. The higher your deductible, the_____ the cost of the insurance.

10. The type of coverage that pays for damages caused by mother nature is _____ physical damage.

12. The amount of the claim that is paid first by the insurance holder is called the _____.

Chapter 5: Stocks and Bonds

Types of Stocks

The ownership of a corporation is divided into transferable units known as **shares of stock**. There are several categories or classes of stock. Individuals and companies buy stocks because they expect to profit when the corporation profits. Corporations issue two basic types of stock: **common stock** and **preferred stock**.

Corporations differ from other types of business structures, such as **sole proprietorships** and **partnerships**. In sole proprietorships, only one person shares in the profits and losses. In partnerships, only the partners share in the financial gains and losses. In a corporate structure, hundreds, thousands, and sometimes even millions of stockholders share the profits and losses. Further, stockholders may buy and sell shares without interfering with the activities of the corporation. There are millions of transactions that occur daily on stock exchanges, and they are independent transactions between buyers and sellers that do not affect the operations of the corporations involved. This is in contrast to sole proprietorships and partnerships, where the life of the business ceases when ownership changes.

One other important distinction between a corporation and the other types of business structures is that investors (stockholders) in a corporation limit their losses to the amount that they invest in shares in case the company gets into serious financial difficulties.

Common Stocks

Common stocks are ownership shares in a corporation. They are sold initially by the corporation and are then traded among investors. Investors who buy them expect to earn **dividends** as their part of the profits, and they also hope that the price of the stock will go up so their investment will be worth more in the future. Common stocks offer no financial guarantees, but over time they have traditionally produced a better return than other investments.

The risks investors take when they buy stocks are that the individual company will not do well or that stock prices in general will weaken. At worst, it is possible to lose an entire investment, though it is not possible to lose more than that. Shareholders are not responsible for corporate debts.

When a corporation sells shares, it gives up some control to investors, whose primary concerns are profits and dividends. In return for this scrutiny, the company gets investment money it needs to build or expand the business.

Preferred Stocks

Preferred stocks are also ownership shares issued by a corporation and traded by investors. They differ from common stocks in several ways that reduce the investor risk, but that may also limit profits. The amount of the dividend is guaranteed and paid before dividends on common stock. However, the dividend is not increased if the company profits increase or if the price of the preferred stock increases. One advantage is that, since preferred stock is paid dividends first, owners of preferred stocks have a greater chance of getting some of their investment back if a company should fail.

Stock Splits

When the price of a stock gets too high, investors are often reluctant to buy, either because they think it has reached its peak or because it costs so much. Corporations have the option of splitting the stock to lower the price and stimulate trading. When a stock is split, there are more shares available, but the total market value is the same.

Say a company's stock is trading at $100 a share. If the company declares a two-for-one split, it gives every stockholder two shares for each one held. At the same time, the price drops to $50 a share. An investor who owned 300 shares at $100 now has 600 shares at $50. Notice that the total value is still $30,000.

The initial effect of a stock split is no different than getting change for a dollar; however, there are more shares available at a more affordable price.

Stocks can split three-for-one, three-for-two, ten-for-one, or any other combination. Stocks that have split within the past 52 weeks are identified in *The Wall Street Journal's* stock columns with a $ in the left-hand margin.

Types of Bonds

Bonds are basically loans that investors make to corporations and federal and local governments. The borrowers get the cash they need while the lenders earn interest. It is similar to the investors acting like many small banks lending money to corporations and governments.

There are several reasons why Americans have more money invested in bonds than in the stock market. First, bonds pay a predetermined amount of interest on a regular basis. Further, the issuer (borrower) promises to repay the loan in full and on time. Consequently, bonds tend to be a less risky investment than stocks.

Every bond has a fixed **maturity date** when the bond expires and the loan must be paid back in full. The interest a bond pays is also set when the bond is issued. The interest rate is competitive, which means that the bond pays interest comparable to what investors can earn elsewhere. As a result, the rate on a new bond is usually similar to other current interest rates, including mortgage rates. If the issuer fails to meet the terms of the agreement, then they will receive a poor credit rating, which means the next time they want to issue a bond, people will not likely buy it, even if it pays an above-average interest rate. There are three major types of bonds, and they are discussed on the following page.

Corporate Bonds

Corporations may use the money raised with bonds for many different things. Typically, corporations use bonds to raise capital to pay for modernization or expansion projects, such as new buildings and equipment. They may also use the money to cover operating expenses. In addition, they may use the newly-raised capital to finance corporate takeovers and mergers.

U.S. Treasury Bonds

Unlike companies, governments are not profit-making enterprises and cannot issue stock. Bonds are the primary way governments raise money to fund capital improvements like roads or airports. Money from bond issues may also be used to cover everyday operating expenses when other revenue (taxes) is not sufficient to their costs. Further, the U.S. government may issue bonds and use the money to restructure and pay off other debts.

Municipal Bonds

Municipal bonds are issued by state, county, and city governments. They use the bond money to pay for a wide variety of public projects, such as schools, highways, stadiums, sewage systems, and bridges. The local government units may also use bond money to supplement their operating expenses.

Money is like muck, not good except it be spread. —Francis Bacon

---

Name_____ Date _____

Chapter 5: Student Activities

GUEST SPEAKER IDEA

Have a local stock broker come to class and further explain stocks and the marketplace. Also have the broker explain how to read the stock reports in *The Wall Street Journal.*

STUDENT ACTIVITIES

1. A corporation has 1,000 shares of preferred stock and 5,000 shares of common stock, and the preferred stock has a prior claim to an annual $5 dividend. The annual profits to be distributed for the first three years were $15,000, $25,000, and $4,000, respectively. Calculate how much would be distributed to preferred stock and common stock. Also, calculate the dividends per share.

	First Year	**Second Year**	**Third Year**
Preferred Stock	_____	_____	_____
Common Stock	_____	_____	_____
Dividend Per Share			
Preferred Stock	_____	_____	_____
Common Stock	_____	_____	_____

2. If the ACME corporation has 100,000 shares of common stock issued with a market value of $80 per share and they declare a two-for-one stock split:

   a. How many shares are there now? _____

   b. What is the current value per share after the split?_____

   c. What was the total market value of shares before the split?_____

   d. What is the total market value of shares after the split?_____

3. If the Box corporation has 200,000 shares of common stock issued with a market value of $90 per share and they declare a three-for-one stock split:

   a. How many shares are issued now? _____

   b. What is the current market value per share after the split?_____

   c. What was the total market value of shares before the split?_____

   d. What is the total market value of shares after the split?_____

Name_____ Date _____

Chapter 5: Crossword Puzzle

Use the clues on page 41 to complete the crossword puzzle below about stocks and bonds.

Name_____ Date _____

Chapter 5: Crossword Puzzle Clues

Use the clues below to complete the crossword puzzle on page 40. Answers may be found in the chapter about stocks and bonds.

ACROSS

2. A benefit of being a stockholder is that your losses are limited to your _____.

6. Two basic types of stock are common and_____.

10. When corporations sell stock, they give up some managerial_____.

11. A business entity where a few owners share the profits is called a _____.

13. The dividend of preferred stock is _____.

14. When ownership changes in a sole proprietorship or partnership, the life of the business_____.

16. A business entity where hundreds or thousands of owners share the profits is called a _____.

18. Dividends on preferred stock are paid _____.

19. Investors buy stock with the hope they will earn _____.

DOWN

1. Americans invest more in_____ than in other investments.

3. To stimulate stock trading, a corporation can reduce the stock price via a stock _____.

4. When a stock splits, the total_____ value remains the same.

5. Traditional stocks have produced better _____ than other investments.

6. A business entity where only one owner receives the profits is called a sole _____.

7. The place where stock transactions take place is called the stock _____.

8. Corporations issue stock to raise _____.

9. A disadvantage of preferred stock is that when profits increase, dividends remain the _____.

12. In a sole proprietorship, the owner is subject to unlimited _____.

15. Ownership of a corporation comes in the form of transferable units known as shares of _____.

17. Corporate dividends are part of the business' _____.

Chapter 6: Buying An Automobile and Major Household Goods

In the very near future, most of us will be in the market for a new or used automobile. For most buyers, whether first-time or experienced buyers, this is an exciting time. Just the idea of getting something new usually gets buyers excited, let alone a new automobile. This new car will further describe who the buyer is. Is he or she a sporty person with a two-seat convertible, or a powerful person with a muscle car and loud exhaust system? Or perhaps the owner is a party person with a van and the ideal stereo, or maybe they are the rugged type with a four-wheeling pick-up truck. We get to make some great personal decisions like: Should the car have chrome wheels? Raised letter tires? What color should it be? What type of music system and how many speakers?

We can really get caught up in the car-purchasing process. This is just what your local car salespeople are counting on. They are more than willing to accommodate your every desire, because every additional option you desire means more **commission** for them. This means that the amount of money they make depends on how much they sell. Plus, the more you are emotionally attached to the prospective car, the more you are willing to pay for it. The same holds true for major household goods like furniture, computers, and appliances.

Experienced salespeople see many emotionally-charged buyers every day and know exactly how to feed their desires. They know exactly the right thing to say and the right time to say it, to encourage your emotional attachment to one of the most important purchases in your life—a purchase you will have to live with for many years, even if you have not realized this yet.

It is important that we realize that, as consumers, we are far too impulsive to patiently apply our common sense and wisdom when we are shopping for **consumer durable goods**, such as furniture, computers, appliances, and automobiles. If we recognize our human weakness initially, we can prepare ourselves and be much smarter consumers. It is important that we make ALL the important decisions about the type and options needed before we go to the store and get caught up in the shopping frenzy. We will focus our discussion on automobiles, but the same logic applies to other major household goods as well.

By pre-thinking our purchase, we may be taking some of the fun and excitement of shopping away from the experience, but we usually save a lot of money and decrease the chance of post-purchase problems. The most important part of this process is that, whatever you decide at home, you cannot let the emotional experience, store atmosphere, or fast-talking salespeople change your mind. If you cannot resist all the marketing temptations that you will be confronted with, then there is little value in going through the pre-thinking process.

The first thing you should do before going to the store and making a major purchase is to research your potential purchase as thoroughly as possible. Good sources for your research will include the newspaper, catalogs, and the Internet. Look at these sources to see what types of prices, choices, and features are available. From your research, you will want to make a written checklist of the following items. Be sure to take this list with you when you go to the store.

Checklist for Major Consumer Purchases

This would include furniture, computers, appliances, and automobiles.

_____ 1. What is the absolute maximum price I will pay for this item?

_____

_____ 2. Is there one brand name that I prefer?

_____

_____ 3. What style am I seeking?

_____

_____ 4. What size requirements do I have?

_____

_____ 5. What features or options must I absolutely have?

_____

_____

_____

_____

_____ 6. What features or option would be a nice bonus, if included?

_____

_____

_____

_____

_____ 7. What features or options am I unsure about and need more information?

_____

_____

_____ 8. Do I need delivery of the item to my home?

_____

_____ 9. Do I need help with installation?

_____

_____ 10. Do I need support help with operation of the purchased item?

_____

_____ 11. Will I need a warranty/extended service plan?

_____

_____ 12. Where will I get this item repaired if necessary?

_____

_____ 13. Does this brand hold its resale value better than other brands?

_____

_____ 14. If financing is needed, can it be obtained, or even better, do I have pre-approval
from a bank or credit union?

_____

_____

_____ 15. Does this purchase fit into my budget?

_____

_____ 16. Will this product still suit my needs in the next few years?

_____

Once you make these decisions, it is important that you stick to them. If, after store shopping, you find you need to re-think your previous decisions, go home and re-think; do NOT second-guess yourself at the store or under the presure of a salesperson.

> Too many of us are spending money we haven't earned to buy things we don't need to impress people we don't like. —Unknown

Name_____ Date _____

Chapter 6: Student Activities

GUEST SPEAKER IDEAS

1. Invite a local college professor of marketing to speak to the class on the use of marketing techniques and tactics used at the retail level to entice consumers to buy. Also, have him or her discuss how advertising and peer group pressure influence buying behavior.

2. Invite a representative from a local bank or credit union to class to discuss consumer loans. Have him or her discuss how he or she determines the amount a customer can borrow, along with how he or she determines the loan value of an automobile.

STUDENT ACTIVITIES

1. Have the students determine what vehicle they would like to purchase after they have obtained their driver's licenses. Have them research the newspapers, Internet, and possibly visit car lots to determine prices and options desired. Have students use the checklist on pages 43–44 in order to crystallize their needs.

2. Based on Activity 1, students should have a fairly good idea of the vehicle they desire, along with the costs involved. For the purposes of this exercise, let's say the student has been able to save up an $800 down payment on the vehicle and needs to finance the remainder. Let's also assume the student has a part-time job and that he or she can afford a $40 monthly car payment. The bank is willing to finance the vehicle for up to three years. Can the student afford the car he or she chose in Activity 1 interest-free? (Multiply the monthly payments by the number of months and then add the down payment. Any car up to that total can be financed interest-free.)

_____

3. To calculate simple interest and payments, use the following formulas:

Principle (amount borrowed) x Time (in years) x Interest rate = Interest

Principle + Interest ÷ # of months of loan = Monthly loan payment

Using the above formulas, solve the following problem. Jill made her best deal on a used car for $3,500. She had $700 to use as a down payment. Jill borrowed the remainder from the bank at six percent interest for three years. What was her monthly car payment?

_____

Name_____ Date _____

Chapter 6: Crossword Puzzle

Use the clues on page 47 to complete the crossword puzzle below about purchasing automobiles and household goods.

Name_____ Date _____

Chapter 6: Crossword Puzzle Clues

Use the clues below to complete the crossword puzzle on page 46. Answers may be found in the chapter about purchasing automobiles and household goods.

ACROSS

1. In the near future, most of us will be looking to buy a new or used _____.

4. Concerns we have after buying a product are called _____ problems. (hyphenated word)

6. Decisions we make ourselves are called _____ decisions.

9. Someone who has bought the product before is considered an_____ buyer.

12. People who buy products for their own personal use are called_____.

13. People tend to get very caught up in the purchasing _____.

14. Consumer products that are intended to last many years are _____ goods.

15. Appliances and furniture are referred to as durable _____ goods.

DOWN

2. The different features you choose for your new car are called_____.

3. The money the salesperson makes from selling a car is called _____.

5. The person you talk to at the car lot is the _____.

7. When buying something new, we tend to get _____.

8. A durable goods purchase is one you will have to live with for many_____.

10. Shopping for durable goods can be an _____ experience.

11. When people buy products without much thought, they are being_____.

Chapter 7: Buying a Home

Know Your Price Range and Related Costs

Buying a home is usually the largest purchase in one's life. It is a very important purchase decision, one that you must literally live with for a long time. Because of the importance of a home purchase, there are several legal aspects to the buying of a home. For this reason, most buyers, especially first-time home buyers, rely on the expertise of realtors and attorneys to help them through the maze of paperwork.

Unless you can pay cash for the house you desire, the first thing you want to do is find a good mortgage lender and find out exactly what your housing price range is. You do not want to waste time looking at homes outside your price range. Begin by asking co-workers, friends, neighbors, or real estate agents to recommend lenders they have had a good experience with. You should talk to at least three lenders and compare the following:

- What is the **interest rate** and the **annual percentage rate** (APR)? The APR is the one figure you can use to compare mortgage lenders' offerings.

- How many **points** does the lender charge? Each point is equal to one percent of the loan amount. Points are charged to cover some of the lender's costs, and sometimes they will offer a lower interest rate if you are willing to pay some points.

- What is the total cost of the **loan fees** and **closing costs**? Make sure you understand who pays for what before it comes time to finalize the deal. Some items are negotiable and some items are not. Typical closing costs would include appraisal fees, attorney fees, realtor fees, termite inspection, and pro-rated taxes, just to name a few.

> Money is always there, but the pockets change. —Stein

Checklist of Basic Information Needed for a Home Loan Application

_____ 1. Checking, Savings, Certificates of Deposit, Money Market, and IRA Accounts
* names and addresses of institutions
* account numbers
* balances

_____ 2. Loans (auto, home, student, other bank and credit union loans, etc.)
* names and addresses of institutions
* monthly payments
* balances and purposes of loans

_____ 3. Credit Cards
* each card's name and name of institution that issued the card
* account numbers
* balances and average monthly payments

_____ 4. Employment Information
* names and addresses of employers for the past five years
* dates of employment

_____ 5. Self-employment
* last five years' personal tax returns
* last five years' corporate or partnership tax returns
* year-to-date profit and loss statements

_____ 6. Real Estate Owned
* value of property
* lease agreement with terms
* names and addresses of lenders
* monthly payments, balances, and account numbers

_____ 7. Personal Assets
* year, model, and value of automobiles, boats, RVs, etc.
* cash value of life insurance
* value of stocks and bonds
* value of jewelry, antiques, etc.

_____ 8. Purchase contract on home being purchased

_____ 9. Listing on home being purchased

_____ 10. Contract on home being sold, if applicable

_____ 11. Recent payroll stubs

_____ 12. Last two years' W-2s for related jobs

_____ 13. Divorce decree/separation agreement, if applicable

_____ 14. Appraisal fee and credit report fee payment

What You Want in a Home

Once you know your price range and related costs, it is time to devise a checklist of what is important to you in a home. You should divide your list into two categories: "Must Have" and "Like to Have" features. This is sometimes very difficult, because the members of a family may not see eye-to-eye on everything. The more time and effort you put into this step, the easier and shorter your home search will be. Here is a list of some common features and frequently overlooked items to include on your checklist.

Checklist of Desired Housing Features

Living Space

_____ * Total square feet

_____ * Number of bedrooms

_____ * Number of bathrooms

_____ * Kitchen (appliances needed)

_____ * Laundry room (appliances needed)

_____ * Family room

_____ * Formal living room

_____ * Formal dining room

_____ * Basement (unfinished/finished)

_____ * Garage (1-, 2-, or 3-car)

_____ * Yard space (basketball hoop, pet area, swimming pool, swing set, etc.)

Utilities

_____ * Type of heat (gas or electric, forced air or radiant heat)

_____ * Type of water heater (gas or electric)

_____ * Air conditioning (yes or no)

_____ * Water (city or well)

_____ * Sewer (city or septic)

_____ * Average monthly utility costs

General Area

_____ * Part of city or county desired

_____ * School district

_____ * Shopping areas (grocery, drug, convenience stores)

_____ * Zoning

_____ * Taxes

_____ * Age of house and neighborhood

Other Considerations

_____ * Driving time to and from work

_____ * Traffic flow to and from work and shopping

_____ * Bussing/driving time to and from school

_____ * Style of home desired

_____ * Distance from your church

_____ * Distance from medical centers (routine and emergencies)

_____ * Is the house east of work? Having the Sun at your back is preferable to
having it in your eyes as you go to and from work.

_____ * Is the home the target of headlights at night?

_____ * Is traffic, factory, or siren noise a potential problem?

_____ * Is neighborhood compatible with your lifestyle (quiet, active, kids, teenagers, married, singles, elder couples, etc.)?

Once you have talked to your financial institution to determine what you can comfortably afford and have done some searching to determine what features you need in your home, then it is time to start looking at houses. Most buyers look at five to twelve homes if they have a good idea of what they are looking for. Your realtor can do a computer search to find homes for sale that match your requirements.

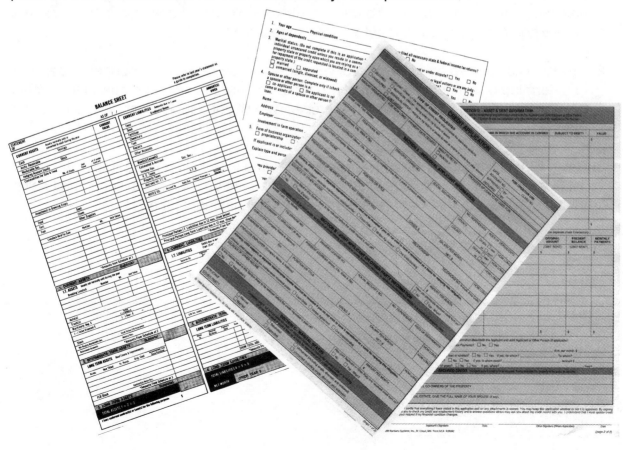

Name_____ Date _____

Chapter 7: Student Activities

GUEST SPEAKER IDEAS

1. Ask a residential realtor to discuss the housing market in your community. Ask the person to describe the services they offer, how they determine both the clients' needs and what they can afford, and how they go about finding the right house for their clients' particular situations.

2. Ask a local attorney who represents home buyers what services his or her firm offers. What things should a prospective home buyer watch out for in a purchase agreement? Does he or she represent his or her clients in price negotiations? If so, does he or she feel that they are more qualified to do this than a realtor?

3. Ask a local housing lender to address how he or she determines how much to loan people for home mortgages. Also, ask him or her to discuss alternative forms of financing, such as second mortgages.

STUDENT ACTIVITIES

1. Fill out the "Checklist of Desired Housing Features." Be specific in number, amount, and size of your dream home. Then, get together in small groups to try to determine how much each group member's dream house would cost. Look in local newspapers or free home magazines distributed by local realtors for prices.

2. After you have determined the cost of your dream house, fill out the budget on page 53 to determine how much you could afford for a monthly payment and how long it would take to pay off your house. For this exercise, we will not add interest payments to the mortgage.

3. Review the "Checklist of Basic Information Needed for a Home Loan Application" and list five things you can do, between now and the time you will actually be purchasing your first house, that will increase your chances of getting loan approval.

4. Complete the "Home Building Activity" on pages 54–56.

Name_____ Date _____

MONTHLY BUDGET

Assume that you make $29,000 a year.

1. Fill out the form below to determine how you would divide your monthly income to pay for the following expenses. Do some research about the cost of the following items, and then estimate your costs.

2. How much could you afford for a monthly payment on your dream house?_____

3. At that rate, how long would it take you to pay for your house?_____

Monthly Income: _____	
Item	**Cost**
Food	
Electricity	
Natural Gas	
Telephone	
Gas for Auto	
Auto Insurance	
Health Insurance	
Life Insurance	
Clothing	
Entertainment	
Miscellaneous	
House Payment	

Name_____ Date _____

HOME BUILDING ACTIVITY

Sometimes you just cannot find the right house in the right location. If that is the case, an option open to you is to have a house built. Using the following two pages, draw to scale the floor plan for the inside of your dream house (bird's eye view) and the front of the house based on your interior design. For this exercise, limit the house to one story with 1,800 square feet of living space and an attached 24 x 24 foot garage. You can include any rooms you like, along with fireplaces, closets, and so on. An example is given below.

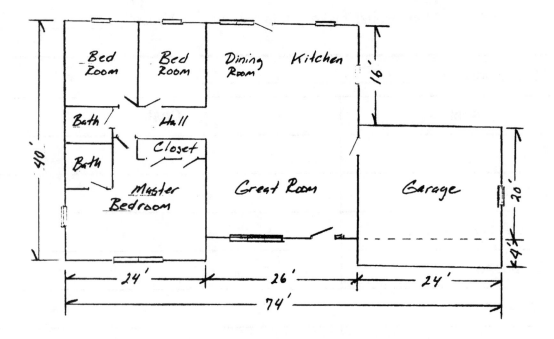

Floor Plan

Front Elevation

Name_____ Date _____

1. INTERIOR HOUSE DESIGN (Floor Plan From a Bird's-Eye View)

1,800 square feet living space with attached 24 x 24 foot garage.

Name_____ Date _____

2. EXTERIOR HOUSE DESIGN (Front Elevation)

Based on interior design.

Name_____ Date _____

Chapter 7: Crossword Puzzle

Use the clues on page 58 to complete the crossword puzzle below about purchasing a home.

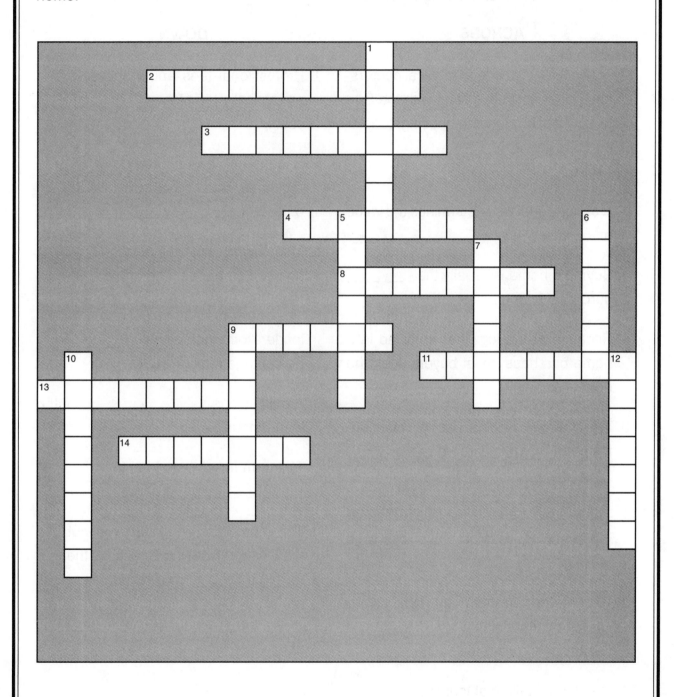

Name_____ Date _____

Chapter 7: Crossword Puzzle Clues

Use the clues below to complete the crossword puzzle on page 57. Answers may be found in the chapter about purchasing a home.

ACROSS

2. Traffic flow, distance to medical centers, and house to work driving with the Sun to your back are some housing considerations that are _____ overlooked.

3. A professional who determines the value of a property is an_____.

4. Buying a home is usually the _____ purchase in one's life.

8. Because of the legalities involved in a home purchase, most buyers seek the help of an _____.

9. The charges lenders use to cover administrative costs are referred to as _____.

11. The two categories in the Desired Housing Checklist are "Must Have" and "Like to Have" _____.

13. Your realtor can help you narrow your search by first doing a _____ search of homes listed.

14. You should talk to at least three _____ to see who has the best financing options.

DOWN

1. Professional fees and inspection fees are typical examples of _____ costs.

5. Because of the importance of a home purchase, most buyers rely on the expertise of a _____.

6. Most buyers look at five to _____ homes before deciding on one.

7. The one figure you can use to compare lenders' offerings is the _____ percentage rate.

9. A point is one _____ of the loan amount.

10. The term for a home loan is _____.

12. The more time and effort you put into the Desired Housing Checklist, the _____ your home search will be.

Chapter 8: Taxes

We have all heard the old adage, "In this life there are only two things that are certain: death and taxes." I don't know about you, but given a choice, I'll take taxes. Some people get very upset upon the mere mention of taxes, while others see taxes as a fact of life. Regardless of your personal view of taxation, our society as we know it could not function without some system of taxation. People constantly demand that the government provide them with various services, such as defense, highways, schools and teachers, unemployment benefits, medical care, and environmental protection, just to name a few. The cost of providing these services that are requested by the citizens of the United States is covered by tax money received by the government. Learning to deal with taxes, and perhaps using them to your advantage, is an essential element of success in today's world.

The federal income tax is a sophisticated and complex array of laws that imposes a tax on the income of individuals, corporations, estates, and trusts. Current tax law has developed over a period of more than 80 years through a dynamic process involving political, economic, and social forces. At this very minute, Congress is considering various changes in the tax law; the Internal Revenue Service (IRS) and the courts are issuing new interpretations of current tax laws, and professional tax advisers are working to determine the meanings of all these changes.

DEFINITION OF A TAX

What is a tax and what is not a tax? **The IRS defines a tax as** "an enforced contribution, in accordance with legislative authority in the exercise of the taxing power, and imposed and collected for the purpose of raising revenue to be used for public or governmental purposes. Taxes are not payments for some special privilege granted or service rendered."

In everyday terminology, a **tax** could be viewed as an involuntary contribution required by law to finance the functions of government.

There are four characteristics to the IRS definition of taxes that distinguish them from other payments made to government agencies.

1. The payment to the governmental authority is required by law.

2. The payment is required in accordance with the legislative power to tax.

3. The purpose of requiring the payment is to provide revenue to be used for public or governmental purposes.

4. Special benefits, services, or privileges are not received as a result of making the payment. The payment is not a fine or penalty that is imposed under the powers of government.

Although the IRS definition states that the payment of a tax does not provide the taxpayer with directly measurable benefits, the taxpayer does benefit from, among other things, military security, a legal system, and a relatively stable political, economic, and social environment.

Certain payments that look like a tax are not considered a tax under the IRS definition. For example, an annual licensing fee paid to a state to engage in a specific occupation, such as medicine, law, or accounting is not a tax because the payment provides a direct benefit to the payer of the fee. A fee paid for driving on a toll road, the quarter deposited in a parking meter, and payment to a city for water and sewer services are not a tax because, again, the payment provides a direct benefit to the payer. Fines and penalties are generally imposed to discourage behavior that is harmful to the public interest and not to raise revenue to finance government operations. Thus, fines for violating public laws and penalties on tax returns are not taxes.

TYPES OF TAXES

Federal, state, and local governments use a variety of taxes to fund their operations. An examination of the sources of tax revenue shows that the bulk of the federal government's revenue comes from the income tax and social security tax. State and local governments also receive a substantial portion of their revenues from income tax, sales tax, and property tax. There are many other taxes individuals pay, but the ones mentioned above account for the vast majority of tax revenue for federal, state, and local governments.

Income Taxes

The federal government collects a tax on the income of individuals, corporations, estates, and trusts. Most states also tax the incomes of these same groups, and a few local governments also impose an income tax on those who work or live within their boundaries. In its simplest form, **taxable income** is the difference between the total income of a taxpayer and the deductions allowed to that taxpayer. Thus, the study of income taxation is really the study of what must be reported as income and what is allowed as a **deduction** from that income to arrive at the taxable income.

Each of the three government units that impose an income tax has its own set of rules for determining what is included in income and what is deductible from income to arrive at the taxable income. We will limit our discussion to federal income tax procedures because it is the same for everyone, regardless of where they live. Each state and county has its own special taxing procedures.

Income taxes are determined on an annual basis. However, the United States uses a pay-as-you-go collection system under which taxpayers pay an estimate of their tax as they earn their income. Employers must withhold income taxes from wages and salaries of their employees and remit them on a timely basis to the appropriate government body. When taxpayers file their tax returns, these prepaid amounts are credited against their actual bill, resulting in either a refund of overpaid taxes or an additional tax due if not enough tax has been withdrawn. Self-employed taxpayers are not subject to withholding but must make quarterly estimated tax payments that are applied against their tax bill upon the filing of the return.

Income Tax Forms

Each year employers must give employees copies of forms that indicate how much money has been withheld throughout the year and sent to the federal government as income tax and Social Security tax. The **W-2 form** is issued to anyone who is a regular employee on the payroll of a business, such as a student who works part-time at a restaurant or department store. The **1099-Misc form** is issued to anyone who has miscellaneous income from a business, but is not on the regular payroll, such as a student who occasionally shovels snow or mows the lawn for a business. Examples of these forms are shown below.

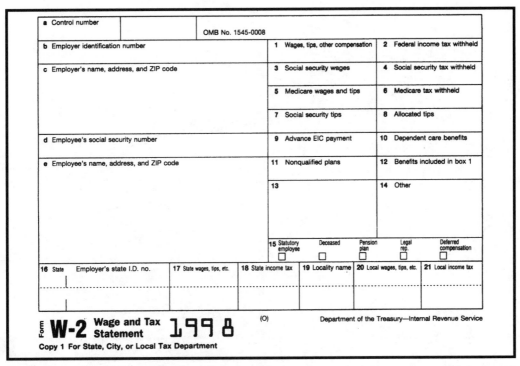

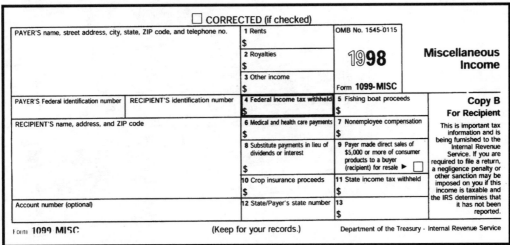

In addition to federal income taxes, employees must pay state income taxes. Employers withhold this money from a person's salary, just as they do with federal taxes. Every state has its own state income tax forms that people who work in the state must file. Examples are shown below.

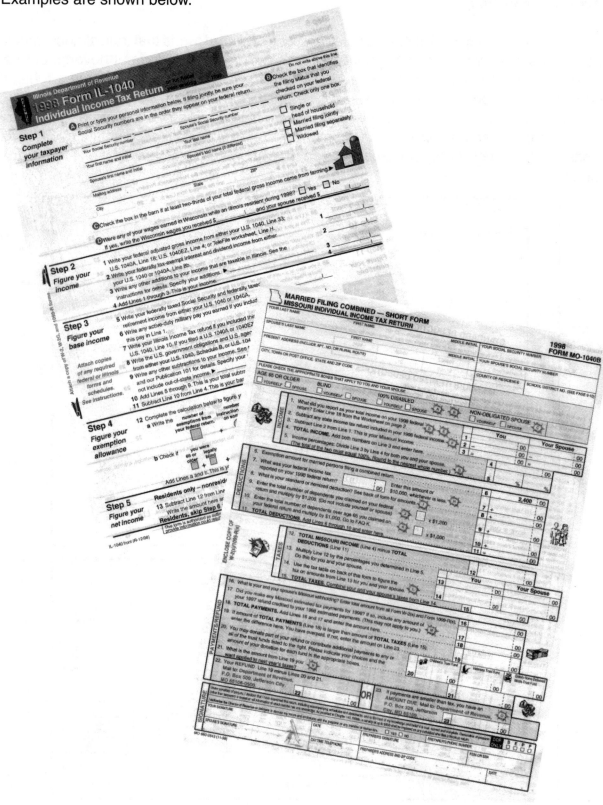

Employment Taxes

All employees and their employers pay taxes on the wages earned by employees. Employees pay **Social Security taxes** that are matched by their employers. Self-employed individuals pay the total of both halves of the Social Security tax by paying the **self-employment tax**. In addition to the Social Security tax, employers pay unemployment compensation taxes to both the federal and state governments.

Social Security Taxes—Under the Federal Insurance Contribution Act (FICA), a tax is collected on wages and salaries earned. The Social Security system was originally designed to provide retirement benefits to all individuals who contributed to the system. This system has been expanded to include many other social programs, such as medical insurance, disability benefits, and survivor's benefits. The result of this expansion of coverage has been a great increase in the amount of Social Security taxes paid by workers and employers. It should be noted that the Social Security system is **not** a funded system. Current payments into the system are used to pay current benefits, which are greater than current receivers put into the system. There is no absolute guarantee that the amounts paid by current taxpayers will actually be available to them when they are eligible to receive their benefits. This is an issue that Congress will wrestle with for a long time.

The Social Security tax is imposed on employees and self-employed individuals. Employers are required to match employees' payments into the system. Because a self-employed person is both an employee and an employer, the self-employment tax rate is twice the employee tax, which results in an equal payment of tax by employee/employer and the self-employed.

Unemployment Taxes—Employers must also pay state and federal unemployment taxes on wages paid to employees to fund unemployment benefits. Unemployment taxes do not have to be paid for employees who earn less than $1,500 per calendar quarter, and unemployment tax is not paid on specific agricultural workers.

Sales Tax

Many state and local governments raise significant amounts of revenue from a sales tax. A **sales tax** is based on a flat percentage of the selling price of a product or service. In contrast to income and employment taxes, which are based on the income of taxpayers, a sales tax is based on a taxpayer's consumption of goods and services. The business that sells the goods or services subject to the tax collects the tax for the government. However, the tax is still paid by the taxpayer purchasing the goods or services. Each government unit that imposes a sales tax determines which goods and/or services are subject to the tax. Thus, not all goods and services are subject to a sales tax. For example, medical services are typically exempted from the tax. Other items that are often exempted from the sales tax are food, farm equipment, and sales to tax-exempt (usually not-for-profit) organizations.

Property Taxes

A tax on the value of property owned by taxpayers is called a **property tax**. In general, **real property** is land and any structures that are permanently attached to it, such as buildings. All other types of property are referred to as **personal property**. Because real property is immobile and difficult to conceal from tax assessors, local governments such as cities, counties, and school districts, prefer it as a revenue source.

Property taxes are based on the value of the property being taxed. However, most property taxes are not based on the true fair market value of the property. Rather, the assessed value of the property is used to determine the tax. The assessed value of property varies widely from location to location, but it is typically 50 to 75 percent of the estimated market value of the property. Market values are determined by the designated assessment authority based on various factors such as recent comparable sales, replacement cost per square foot, and other local market conditions.

Taxes on personal property are not as common as taxes on real property. The mobility and ease of concealment of personal property make the collection of a personal property tax administratively difficult. However, automobiles and boats are often assessed a personal property tax as part of their annual licensing fee.

> Taxes are what we pay for civilized society. —Oliver Wendell Holmes, Jr.

Name_____ Date _____

Chapter 8: Student Activities

GUEST SPEAKER IDEA

Have a payroll officer from a local company come and talk to the class about the variety of payroll deductions (including taxes). Also have him or her discuss career opportunities in a payroll department.

STUDENT ACTIVITIES

1. Monroe County just enacted a new law setting a one percent property tax to provide money for the county school system. The one percent tax applies to all property owners in Monroe County. All the public school children will benefit from the tax, even if their parents do not own property. Is the one percent property tax a tax according to the IRS definition?

   Write yes or no and give your reasoning.

   _____

   _____

   _____

   _____

2. Adams County enacted a new tax on the property owners in the Woodbridge neighborhood for a new sewer system. All of the property owners are required to pay the tax and will be automatically connected to the sewer system upon its completion. Is this tax a tax according to the IRS definition?

   Write yes or no and give your reasoning.

   _____

   _____

   _____

   _____

Name_____ Date _____

The social security tax on employees and employers is a constant percentage of wages up to a maximum wage base. Both the percentage and the maximum wage base have been raised over time. As indicated in the table below, the tax has two components. In 1998, a tax of 6.2 percent is levied on the first $68,400 of wages for Old Age, Survivors, and Disability Insurance (OASDI). A tax of 1.45 percent on all wages pays for Medical Health Insurance (MHI).

Year	OASDI	MHI	Total	Maximum Wage Base	Maximum Tax Paid
1994	6.20		6.20	$60,600	$3,757
		1.45	1.45	Wages earned	No maximum
			7.65		
1995	6.20		6.20	$61,200	$3,794
		1.45	1.45	Wages earned	No maximum
			7.65		
1996	6.20		6.20	$62,700	$3,887
		1.45	1.45	Wages earned	No maximum
			7.65		
1997	6.20		6.20	$65,400	$4,055
		1.45	1.45	Wages earned	No maximum
			7.65		
1998	6.20		6.20	$68,400	$4,241
		1.45	1.45	Wages earned	No maximum
			7.65		

3. Bill earned $2,000 during July of 1998 by working construction with his father. How much Social Security tax must Bill and his father's company pay?

_____

4. In 1998, Martha's mother earned a total of $85,000 as a Certified Public Accountant (CPA) for a local law firm. How much Social Security tax does Martha's mother have to pay? How much does her employer have to pay?

_____

Name_____ Date _____

5. The Ball and Chain Corporation owns a piece of land that it purchased for $6,000 in 1995. During the current year, the county assessor determines that the fair market value of the land is $8,000. In the county in which the land is located, assessed values are 50 percent of the fair market value. What is the assessed value of this land?

_____

6. Missouri imposes an annual tag fee on automobiles. The licensing fee is $20. A personal property tax is also levied, based on the initial selling price of the automobile and its age. During 1998, Julie paid a $94 tag fee on her automobile. How much of the fee is a personal property tax?

_____

7. Obtain an instruction booklet for filling out the IRS Form 1040EZ. Assume that you are single and your income is $18,700. You had $220 of taxable interest income. You had $1,075 withheld from your wages for federal income taxes (this would be the amount shown on line 2 of your W-2 form). Using this information, fill out the sample form on page 68.

Do you owe any additional tax? If so, how much? _____

Will you receive a refund? If so, how much?_____

Name_____ Date _____

SAMPLE FEDERAL INCOME TAX FORM (FRONT)

Form 1040EZ	Income Tax Return for Single and Joint Filers With No Dependents	1998

Use the IRS label here

Your first name and initial	Last name

If a joint return, spouse's first name and initial	Last name

Home address (number and street). If you have a P.O. box, see page 7.	Apt no.

City, town or post office, state, and ZIP code. If you have a foreign address, see page 7.

Your social security number

☐☐☐ ☐☐ ☐☐☐☐

Spouse's social security number

☐☐☐ ☐☐ ☐☐☐☐

Presidential Election Campaign (See page 7.)

Note: *Checking "Yes" will not change your tax or reduce your refund.*
Do you want $3 to go to this fund? ► Yes ☐ No ☐

If a joint return, does your spouse want $3 to go to this fund? ► Yes ☐ No ☐

▲ **IMPORTANT!** ▲
You **must** enter your SSN(s) above.

Dollars   Cents

Income

Attach Copy B of Form(s) W-2 here. Enclose, but do not staple, any payment.

1   Total wages, salaries, and tips. This should be shown in box 1 of your W-2 form(s). Attach your W-2 form(s).   1

2   Taxable interest income. If the total is over $400, you cannot use Form 1040EZ.   2

3   Unemployment compensation (se page 8).   3

4   Add lines 1, 2, and 3. This is your **adjusted gross income.** If under $10,030, see page 9 to find out if you can claim the earned income credit on line 8a.   4

Note: *You* **must** *check Yes or No.*

5   Can your parents (or someone else) claim you on their return?
Yes. Enter amount ☐ from worksheet on back
No. If **single**, enter 6,950.00 ☐ If **married**, enter 12,500.00 See back for explanation.   5

6   Subtract line 5 from line 4. If line 5 is larger than line 4, enter 0. This is your taxable income. ► 6

Payments and tax

7   Enter your Federal income tax withheld from box 2 of your W-2 form(s).   7

8a Earned income credit (see page 9).
b   Nontaxable earned income: enter type and amount below.
Type	$
8a

9   Add lines 7 and 8a. These are your total payments.   9

10. Tax. Use the amount on line 6 above to find your tax in the tax table on pages 20-24 of the booklet. Then, enter the tax from the table on this line.   10

Refund
Have it directly deposited! See page 12 and fill in 11b, 11c, and 11d.

11a If line 9 is larger than line 10, subtract line 10 from line 9. This is your refund.   11a

b Routing number ————————————————►
c Type: d Account
   Checking ☐   Savings ☐   Number ↳

Amount you owe

12 If line 10 is larger than line 9, subtract line 9 from line 10. This is the amount you owe. See page 14 for details on how to pay.   12

I have read this return. Under penalties of perjury, I declare that to the best of my knowledge and belief, the return is true, correct, and accurately lists all amounts and sources of income I received during the tax year.

Sign here ▶
Keep copy for your records.

Your signature	Spouse's signature if joint return. See page 7.
Date	Your occupation	Date	Spouse's occupation

For Official Use Only

Name_____ Date _____

Chapter 8: Crossword Puzzle

Use the clues on page 70 to complete the crossword puzzle below about taxes.

Name_____ Date _____

Chapter 8: Crossword Puzzle Clues

Use the clues below to complete the crossword puzzle on page 69. Answers may be found in the chapter about taxes.

ACROSS

2. A tax is an _____ contribution used to finance the functions of government.

5. States and cities raise significant revenue from _____ taxes.

7. Our federal income tax system is sophisticated and _____.

12. Because of the ease of concealment, the collection of _____ property taxes is administratively difficult.

13. The IRS definition of a tax states that the tax does not provide the taxpayer with any directly measurable _____.

14. Penalties and fines are imposed to discourage unfavorable_____.

15. Tax money goes to our_____ so it can provide products and services more economically.

DOWN

1. Employees pay Social Security taxes, and employers must _____ that amount.

3. In the United States taxes are a fact of _____.

4. Social Security is not a funded system because current recipients receive more monetary benefits than they originally _____.

6. The bulk of the federal government's revenue comes from income tax and Social _____tax.

8. Fees paid on a toll road are not taxes because they provide a direct benefit to the _____.

9. Income taxes are determined on an _____basis.

10. Property taxes are based on the _____value of the property.

11. The old adage states, "In this life there are only two things that are certain: death and _____."

Personal Finance Review: Word Search Puzzle

Find and circle the words listed below in the word search puzzle. All the words are associated with personal finance in some way. Words may read forward, backward, horizontally, vertically, or diagonally in the puzzle.

```
P K Y B D E P O S I T S L I P F D K K C
R C R G D O A O S P L I T U T D U T C J
O O U B D I V I D E N D U N L R R S L P
P T J W R P P B O N D S U Q A A A I O G
R S N T P G Y C L T J O K T I C B R S B
I D I A A G E L O S C E C N C E L O I P
E E Y X S B M F S C O F O E O R E T N A
T R L E S C Z Z A C M I T M S U G O G R
O R I S B X T G L O T L S E T T O M E T
R E D I O Z N D E R E L N T I A O D L N
S F O D O I P E S P R A O A P N D E I E
H E B D K N R D E O M S M T O G S R C R
I R A C T C O U C R L R M S I I C U N S
P P E S W O P C U A I E O K N S A S O H
O H O X H M E T R T F V C N T K R N C I
C C B Q B E R I I I E I S A S Z E I E P
E U H D Q X T B T O E N W B T D E N R P
L M O F G F Y L Y N H U Y H E G R U Q H
C S S I A L Q E M C A I N T E R E S T W
T N U O C C A S G N I V A S S W Q M T P
```

BANK STATEMENT
CAREER
COMMON STOCK
DEPOSIT SLIP
INCOME
PASSBOOK
PROPERTY
SALES
SIGNATURE CARD
SPLIT
UNINSURED MOTORIST

BODILY INJURY
CHECKING ACCOUNT
CORPORATION
DIVIDEND
INTEREST
POINTS
PROPRIETORSHIP
SAVINGS ACCOUNT
SOCIAL
TAXES
UNIVERSAL LIFE

BONDS
CLOSING
DEDUCTIBLE
DURABLE GOODS
PARTNERSHIP
PREFERRED STOCK
RECONCILE
SECURITY
SOLE
TERM LIFE

71

Name_____ Date _____

Personal Finance Review: Multiple Choice

Circle the answer that best completes each statement.

1. What people do for a living is called a

    a. hobby   b. career

    c. lifestyle   d. calling

2. If you enjoy what you do for a living, your_____ is high.

    a. salary   b. embarassment

    c. career satisfaction   d. unhappiness

3. To get help from an experienced person in the career you choose, find a(n)

    a. mentor   b. trainee

    c. career counselor   d. intern

4. To put money into your checking account, you must fill out a

    a. signature card   b. deposit slip

    c. check register   d. bank statement

5. The form that helps protect you from losing the money in your checking account to forgery or robbery is called a

    a. signature card   b. deposit slip

    c. check register   d. bank statement

6. A written order to your bank telling the bank to take a certain amount of money from your checking account and pay it to another individual or business is called a

    a. money order   b. stop payment

    c. check   d. pay stub

7. To get your checkbook to agree with your bank statement, you must_____ your checking account.

    a. reorder   b. tabulate

    c. clear   d. reconcile

Name_____ Date _____

8. You will need to remember your secret Personal Identification Number if you want to withdraw money from a(n)

    a. savings account   b. automated teller machine

    c. Internet web site   d. cash register

9. You will need to remember to bring your passbook to the bank if you want to withdraw money from a(n)

    a. savings account   b. automated teller machine

    c. Internet web site   d. cash register

10. Insurance designed to keep one from experiencing major losses of the material things that one has been able to accumulate is called

    a. health insurance   b. life insurance

    c. property insurance   d. accident insurance

11. Insurance designed to help cover lost wages and to pay important expenses in case an unexpected death occurs is called

    a. health insurance   b. life insurance

    c. property insurance   d. accident insurance

12. Ownership shares in a corporation that have a guaranteed dividend are called

    a. common stock   b. split stock

    c. direct stock   d. preferred stock

13. Ownership shares in a corporation that do not offer a financial guarantee, but that traditionally produce a better return than other investments are called

    a. common stock   b. split stock

    c. direct stock   d. preferred stock

14. The date when a bond expires and the loan must be paid back in full is called the

    a. payback date   b. maturity date

    c. interest date   d. bond date

Name_____ Date _____

15. Governments raise a majority of the money to fund capital improvements, such as roads and airports, by issuing

    a. stocks   b. grants

    c. bonds   d. loans

16. Sometimes salespeople are paid based on how much of the product they sell. This is called working on

    a. commission   b. salary

    c. sales results   d. overtime

17. Major household items that are expected to last for several years are called _____ goods.

    a. rugged   b. lifetime

    c. durable   d. appliance

18. To compare mortgage lenders' offerings, you should compare their

    a. closing costs   b. points

    c. annual percentage rates   d. all of the above

19. The difference between the total income of a taxpayer and the deductions allowed to that taxpayer is called the

    a. income tax   b. taxable income

    c. assessment   d. withholding

20. A tax based on a flat percentage of the selling price of a product or service is called a

    a. property tax   b. income tax

    c. employment tax   d. sales tax

Answer Keys

Chapter 1: Student Activites (pages 3–4)

1a. Students can take the right courses in school.

b. Students can expose themselves to situations and experiences that will benefit their career.

2–3. Answers will vary. Teacher check.

Chapter 1: Crossword Puzzle (pages 5–6)

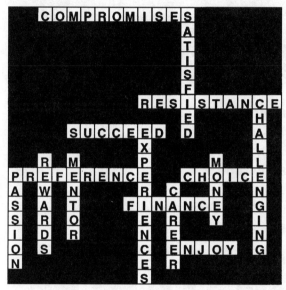

Chapter 2: Review Questions (page 10)

1. At least two of the following: Checks are safer to carry than cash, checks serve as proof of payment, you can establish good credit by properly maintaining your checking accounty, you can keep track of your income and expenses.

2. It helps protect you and your money in case of forgery or robbery. The teller can compare the person's signature to the signature card or ask for personal information.

Let's Practice What We Have Learned (pages 10–12)

1. Teacher check.

2. Teacher check. Total deposit should be $32.50.

3a. four

b. eight

c. ten

d. eleven

e. twelve

f. thirteen

g. fourteen

h. fifteen

i. eighteen

j. nineteen

k. twenty

l. twenty-three

m. thirty

n. thirty-four

o. forty

p. forty-five

q. fifty

r. fifty-six

s. sixty

t. sixty-seven

u. seventy

v. seventy-eight

w. eighty

x. eighty-nine

y. ninety

z. one hundred

aa. one hundred thirteen

bb. seven hundred forty-eight

cc. one thousand

dd. one thousand nine

ee. one thousand seven hundred eighty-three

ff. two thousand

gg. two thousand three hundred thirteen

hh. two thousand nine hundred ninety-nine

4–5. Teacher check.

Chapter 2: Student Activities (pages 15–21)

Teacher check checkbook activity.

Chapter 2: Crossword Puzzle (pages 22–23)

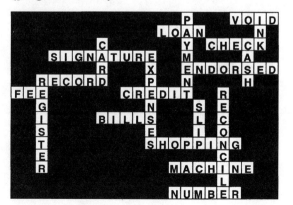

Chapter 3: Student Activities
(pages 25–26)

1. $257.50
   $265.23
   $273.19

2. $265.00
   $280.90
   $297.75

3. $630.00
   $661.50
   $694.58
   $729.31

4. $78.00
   $81.12
   $84.36
   $87.73
   $91.24
   $94.89
   $98.69
   $102.64
   $106.75
   $111.02

5. $205.00
   $315.25
   $431.01
   $552.56
   $680.19

Chapter 3: Crossword Puzzle
(pages 27–28)

Chapter 4: Student Activities (pages 32–33)

Personal Property Inventories will vary. Teacher check.

Chapter 4: Crossword Puzzle
(pages 34–35)

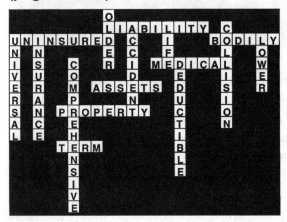

Chapter 5: Student Activities (page 39)

1.	First Year	Second Year	Third Year
Pref:	$5,000	$5,000	$4,000
Com:	$10,000	$20,000	$0
Dividend per Share			
Pref:	$5	$5	$4
Com:	$2	$4	$0

2a. 200,000
  b. $40
  c. $8,000,000
  d. $8,000,000

3a. 600,000
  b. $30
  c. $18,000,000
  d. $18,000,000

Chapter 5: Crossword Puzzle (pages 40–41)

Chapter 6: Student Activities (page 45)
2.
$40 x 12 x 3 = $1,440 + $800 = $2,240
The student can afford a car up to $2,240.
3.
$3,500 - $700 = $2,800 (principal)
$2,800 x 0.06 x 3 = $504 (interest)
$2,800 + $504 = $3,304 (total of loan)
$3,304 ÷ 36 = $92 (monthly payment)

Chapter 6: Crossword Puzzle (pages 46–47)

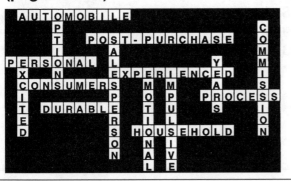

Chapter 7: Student Activities (pages 52–56)
Answers will vary. Teacher check activities.

Chapter 7: Crossword Puzzle (pages 57–58)

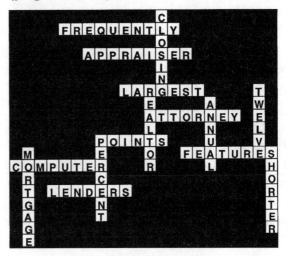

Chapter 8: Student Activities (pages 65–67)
1. The property tax is a tax. The tax is a required payment to a government unit. The payment is imposed by a property tax law. The purpose of the payment is to finance public schools. The tax is levied without regard to whether the taxpayer receives a benefit from paying the tax.

2. Each payer of the tax receives a direct benefit—a new sewer line. Therefore, the one percent tax payment is considered a payment to the government unit to reimburse it for improvements to the taxpayer's property. The taxpayers would treat the payment as an investment in their property and not as a tax. The one percent tax in this case is a special assessment for local benefits. An assessment differs from a tax in that an assessment is levied only on a specific group of taxpayers who receive the benefit of the assessment.

3. Bill must pay 6.2 percent (OASDI) and 1.45 percent (MHI) on the first $68,400 of income earned in 1998. Thus, Bill must pay $153 ($2,000 x 6.2%) + ($2,000 x 1.45%) in Social Security taxes on his wages. The company must match the $153 in Social Security taxes Bill paid on the wages.

4. Mom pays the maximum OASDI of $4,241 (6.2% x $68,400) and $1,233 (1.45% x $85,000) of MHI for a total Social Security payment of $5,474. Her employer is required to pay the same amount on her behalf.

5. The corporation's assessed value is $4,000 ($8,000 x 50%). Note that the local authority can increase or decrease property taxes on the land by varying the percentage of fair market value that is subject to tax. Thus, if the county raised the percentage to 75 percent, the corporation would pay property tax based on an assessed value of $6,000 ($8,000 x 75%).

6. Jule's personal property tax on the automobile is $74 ($94 - $20). The $20 licensing fee is not a tax.

7. Teacher check. Answers will vary according to which year's tax schedule is used.

Chapter 8: Crossword Puzzle (pages 69–70)

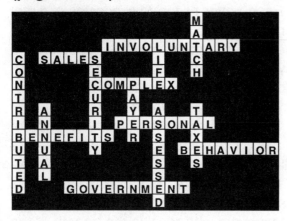

Personal Finance Review: Word Search Puzzle (page 71)

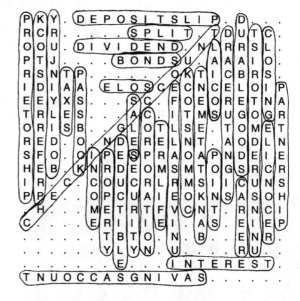

Personal Finance Review: Multiple Choice (pages 72–74)

1. b
2. c
3. a
4. b
5. a
6. c
7. d
8. b
9. a
10. c
11. b
12. d
13. a
14. b
15. c
16. a
17. c
18. d
19. b
20. d